Moonlight Confessions

Elizabeth Grundin

PAGE PUBLISHING
Conneaut Lake, PA

First originally published by Page Publishing 2022

ISBN 979-8-88654-853-2 (pbk)
ISBN 979-8-88654-862-4 (digital)

Printed in the United States of America

Just looking for that spark,
searching for that blazing arc.
Scanning the dark, but it's
looking rather stark.
Then I start to feel the burn mark,
start hearing that smart remark.
I reach out like a reflex arc,
against your caustic remark.
You evade me so easily
'cause I'm an easy mark.
You track me like a merc,
in hopes of leaving another mark.
All the while we are nothing more than
strangers in the dark…

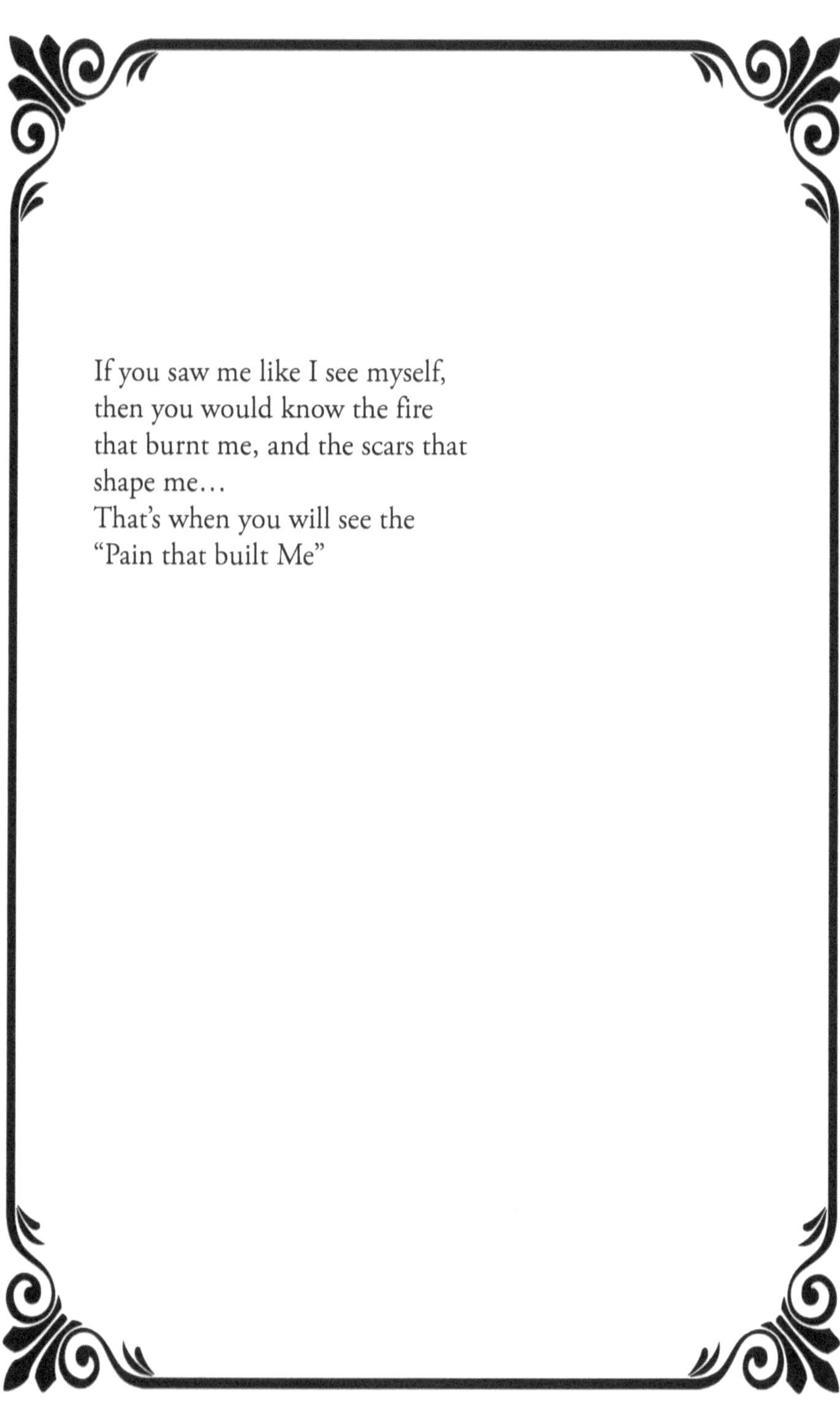

If you saw me like I see myself,
then you would know the fire
that burnt me, and the scars that
shape me…
That's when you will see the
"Pain that built Me"

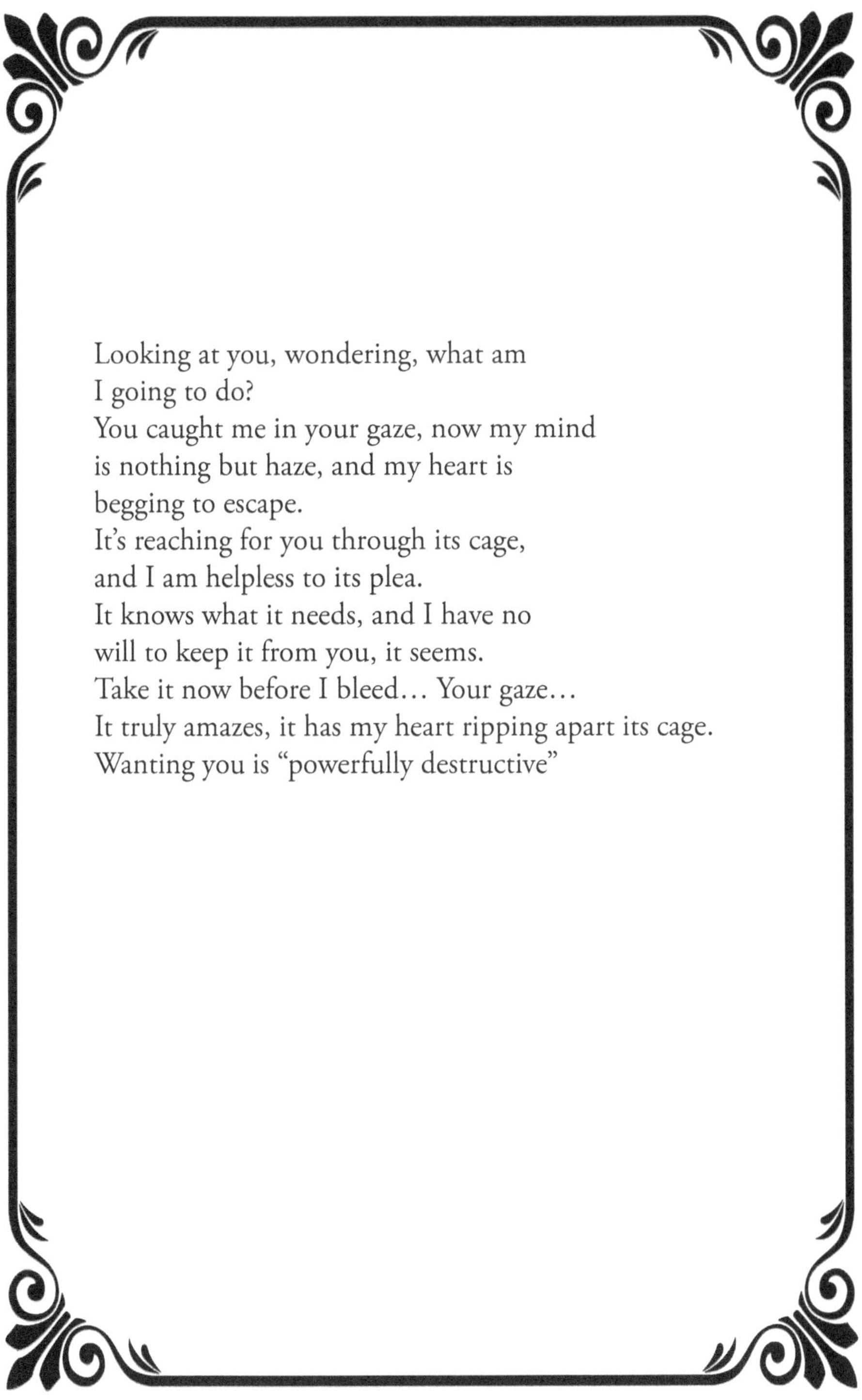

Looking at you, wondering, what am
I going to do?
You caught me in your gaze, now my mind
is nothing but haze, and my heart is
begging to escape.
It's reaching for you through its cage,
and I am helpless to its plea.
It knows what it needs, and I have no
will to keep it from you, it seems.
Take it now before I bleed… Your gaze…
It truly amazes, it has my heart ripping apart its cage.
Wanting you is "powerfully destructive"

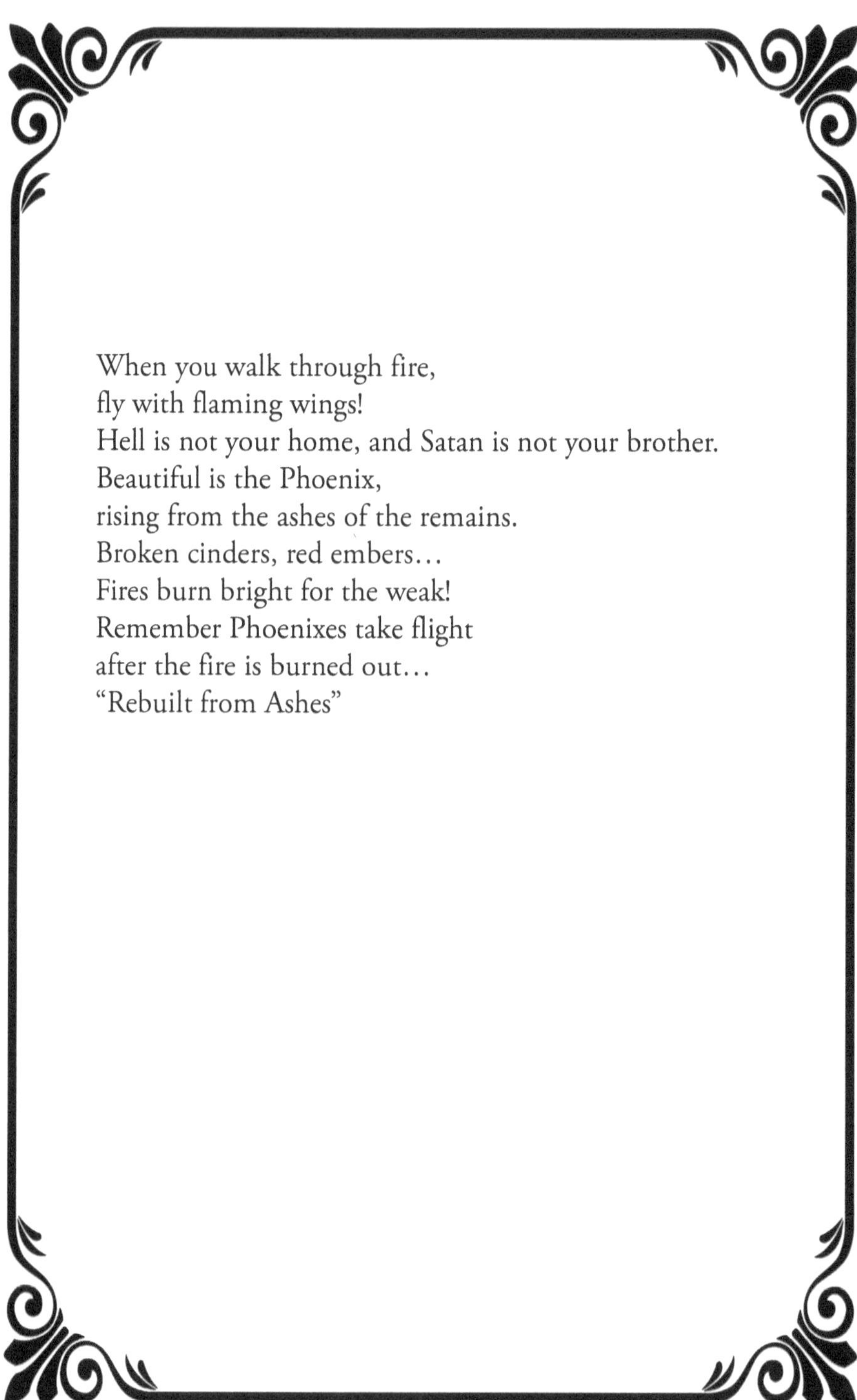

When you walk through fire,
fly with flaming wings!
Hell is not your home, and Satan is not your brother.
Beautiful is the Phoenix,
rising from the ashes of the remains.
Broken cinders, red embers…
Fires burn bright for the weak!
Remember Phoenixes take flight
after the fire is burned out…
"Rebuilt from Ashes"

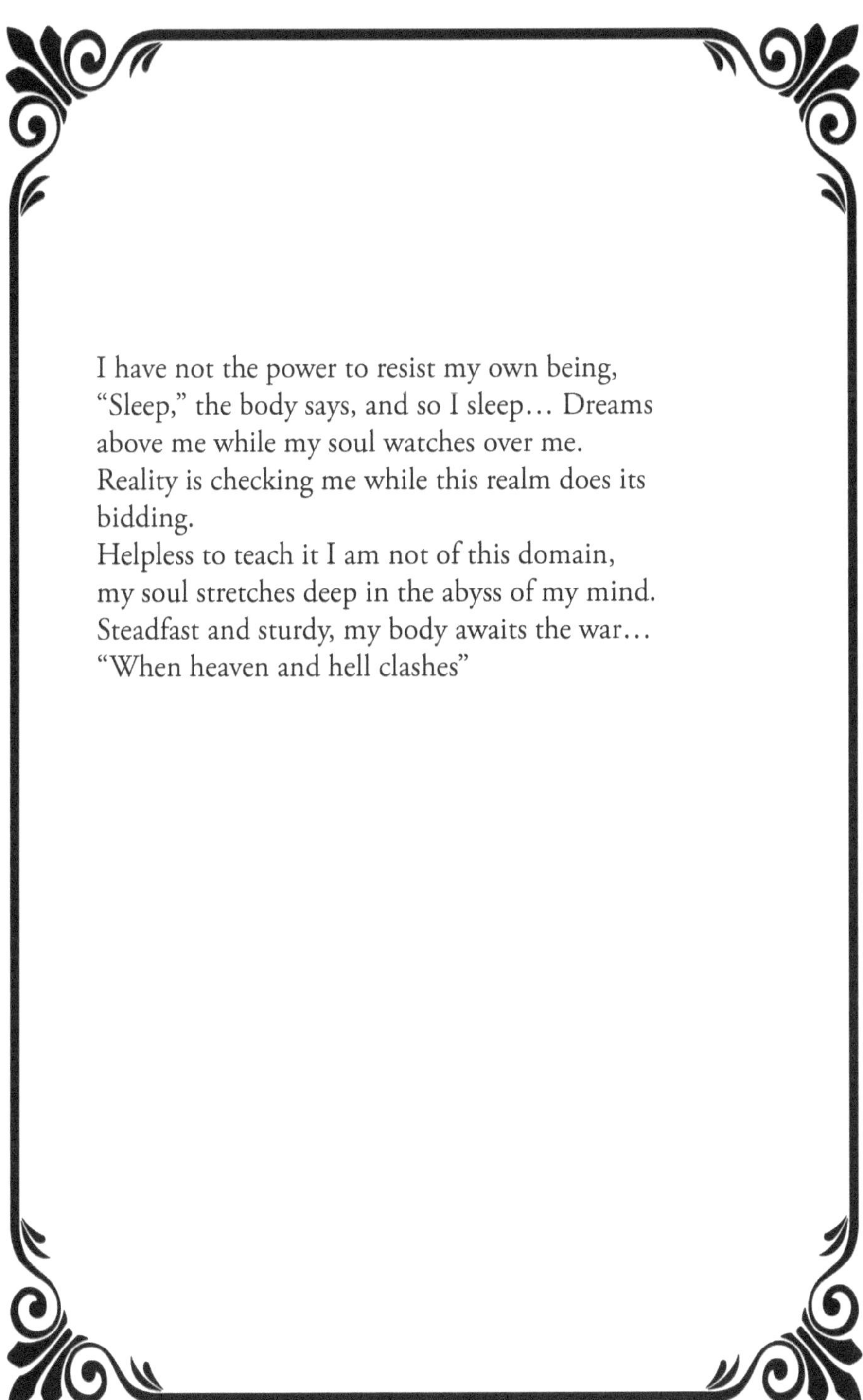

I have not the power to resist my own being,
"Sleep," the body says, and so I sleep… Dreams
above me while my soul watches over me.
Reality is checking me while this realm does its
bidding.
Helpless to teach it I am not of this domain,
my soul stretches deep in the abyss of my mind.
Steadfast and sturdy, my body awaits the war…
"When heaven and hell clashes"

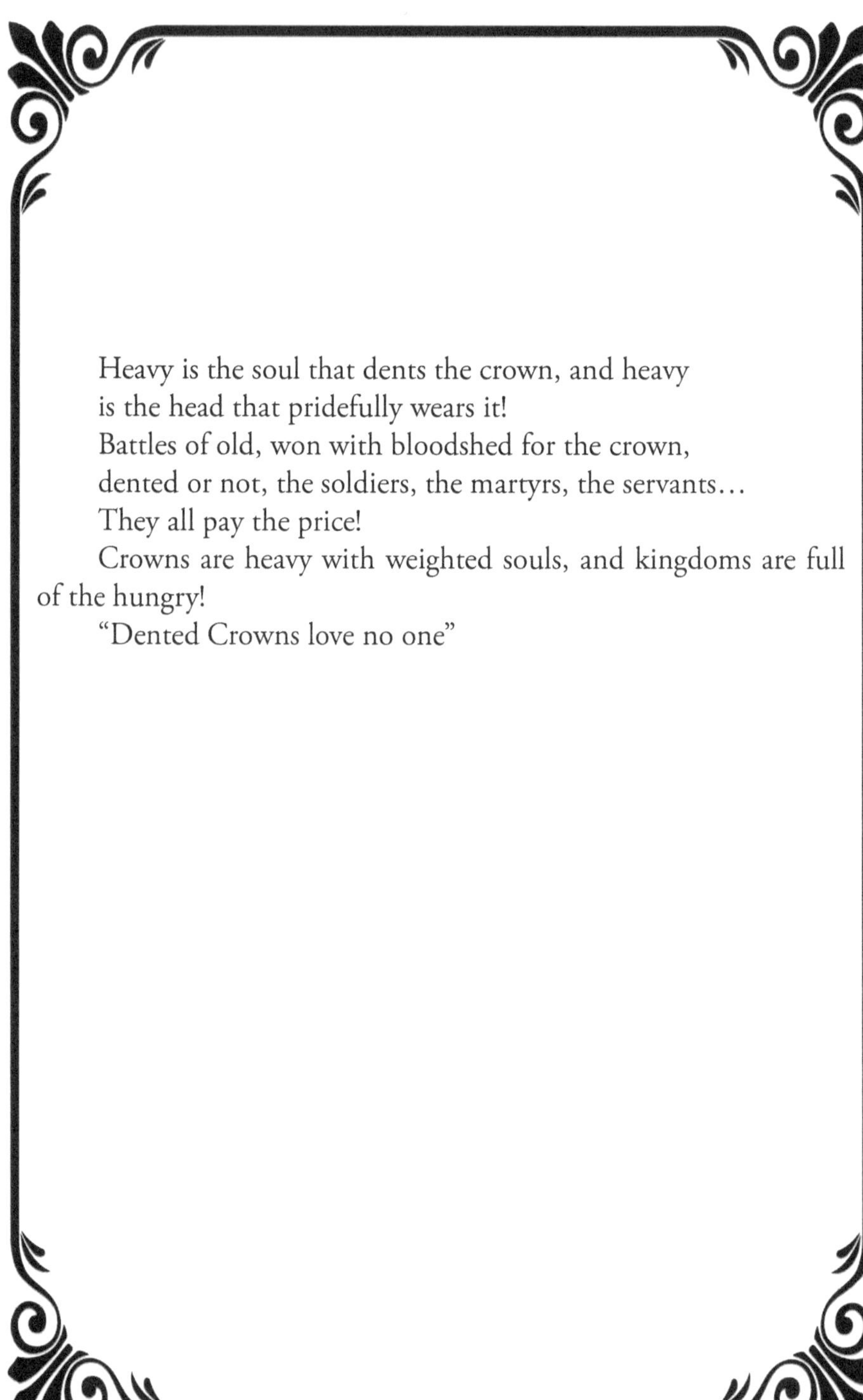

Heavy is the soul that dents the crown, and heavy
is the head that pridefully wears it!
Battles of old, won with bloodshed for the crown,
dented or not, the soldiers, the martyrs, the servants…
They all pay the price!
Crowns are heavy with weighted souls, and kingdoms are full
of the hungry!
"Dented Crowns love no one"

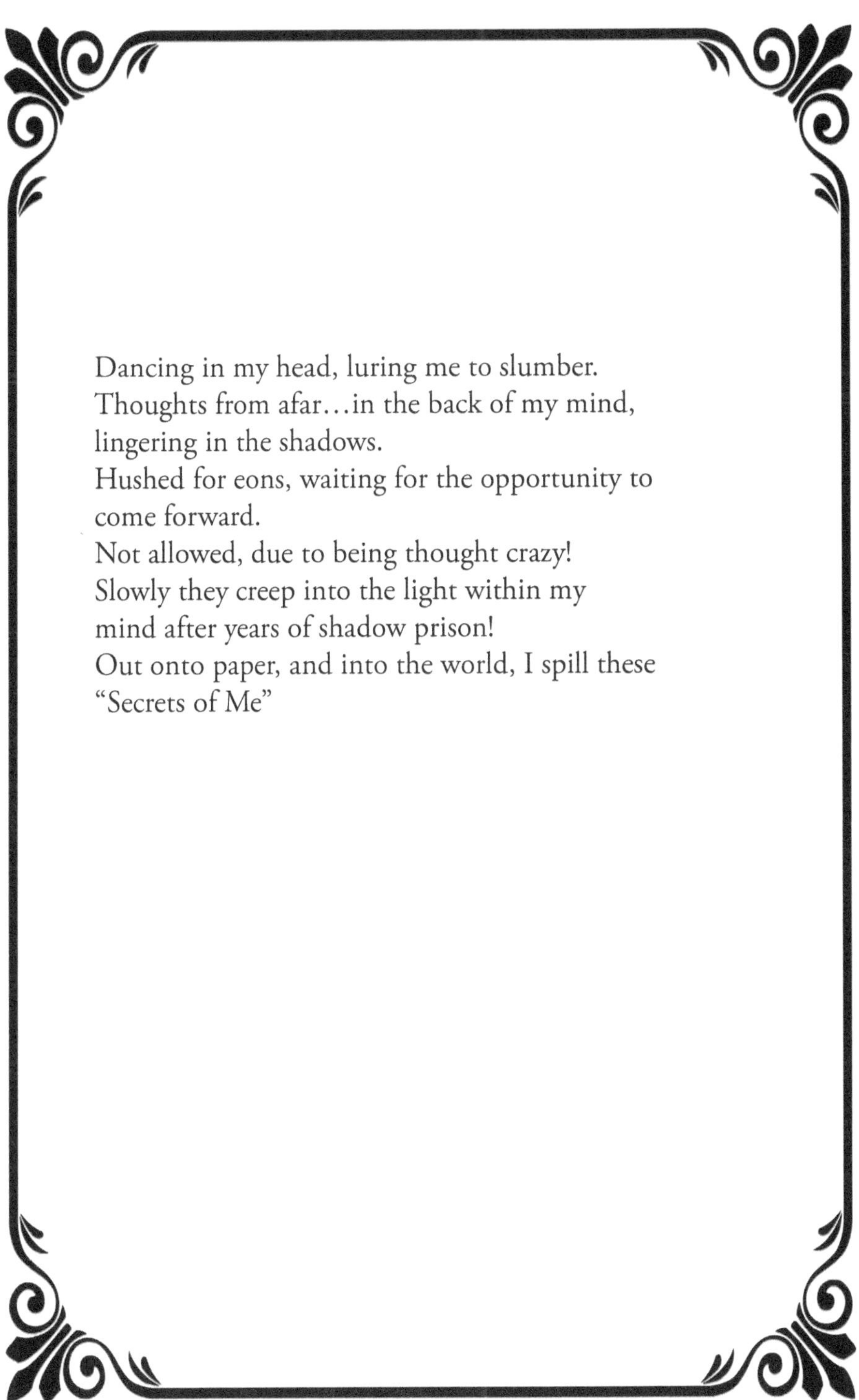

Dancing in my head, luring me to slumber.
Thoughts from afar…in the back of my mind,
lingering in the shadows.
Hushed for eons, waiting for the opportunity to
come forward.
Not allowed, due to being thought crazy!
Slowly they creep into the light within my
mind after years of shadow prison!
Out onto paper, and into the world, I spill these
"Secrets of Me"

As I wake, the emotions take their dues,
heavy with tears, my mind whirls inside my head.
This no one sees.
Waiting as the tears roll down my face, patiently
for my mind to stop just so I can grasp my thoughts.
Heavy is my head, weighing on my soul!
These mornings really get me…
"With all my Violent Strength"

I don't write love songs through tattered winded sails, that seeps through the holes and floats upon the seas.

My life is like a full-blown mountain the likes of Mount Rushmore.

Full of detail, engraved upon my soul, that shines from my eyes like a clear blue summer's day.

All in a day's work, I write these effigies…

"Statues on Paper"

Falling fast, I reach out in hopes of grasping something, anything…almost in panic as I descend into the abyss of my mind… dark as night and dead still!

I breathe slowly waiting for the onslaught of thoughts that crash like waves wreaking havoc against my skull…from one side to the other in a whirlwind of trauma!

Slow, breathe, slow…willing myself to calm…

From the outside, I look fine, while the inside is at war! "Invisible" am I, my name is "Anxiety"

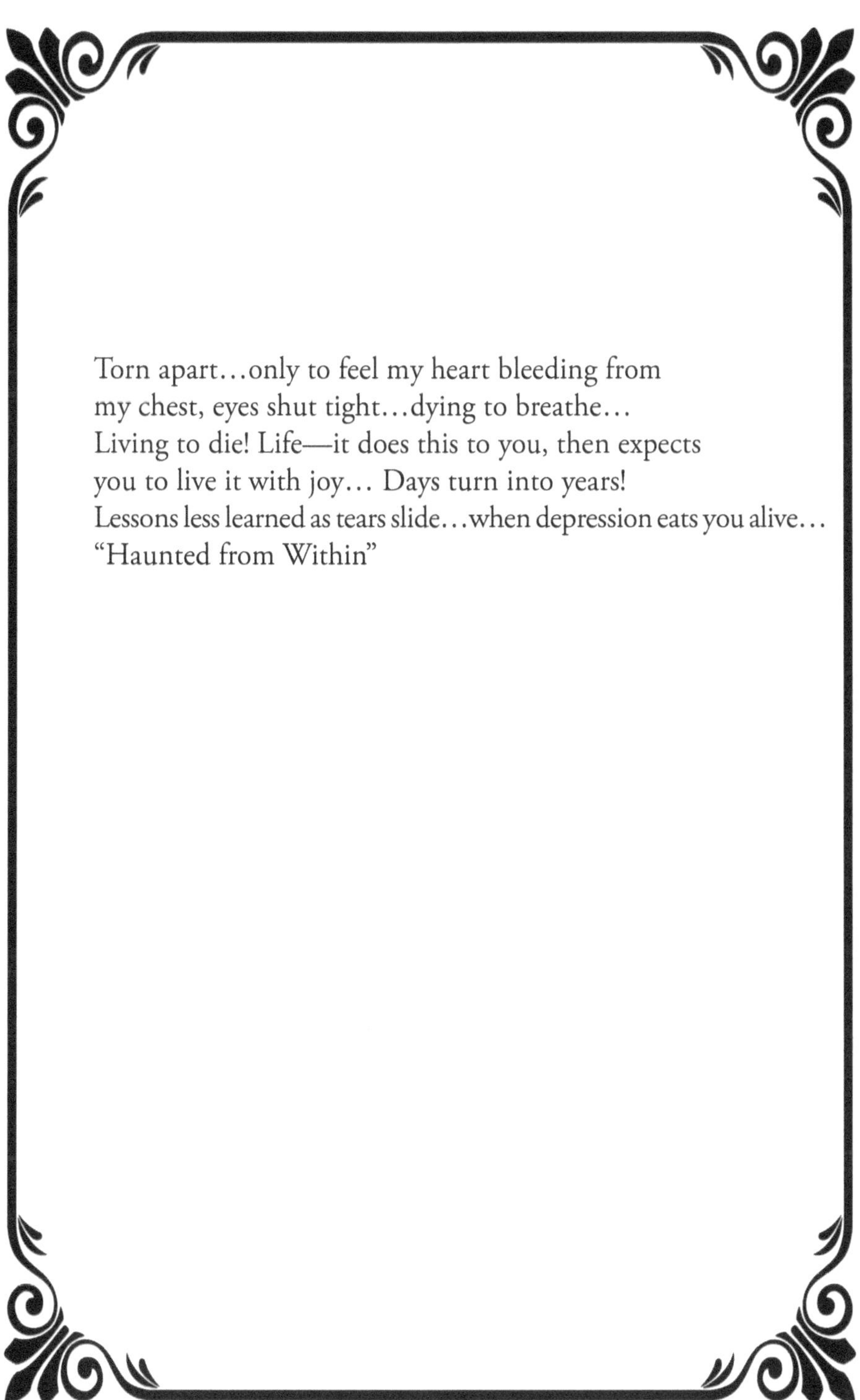

Torn apart…only to feel my heart bleeding from
my chest, eyes shut tight…dying to breathe…
Living to die! Life—it does this to you, then expects
you to live it with joy… Days turn into years!
Lessons less learned as tears slide…when depression eats you alive…
"Haunted from Within"

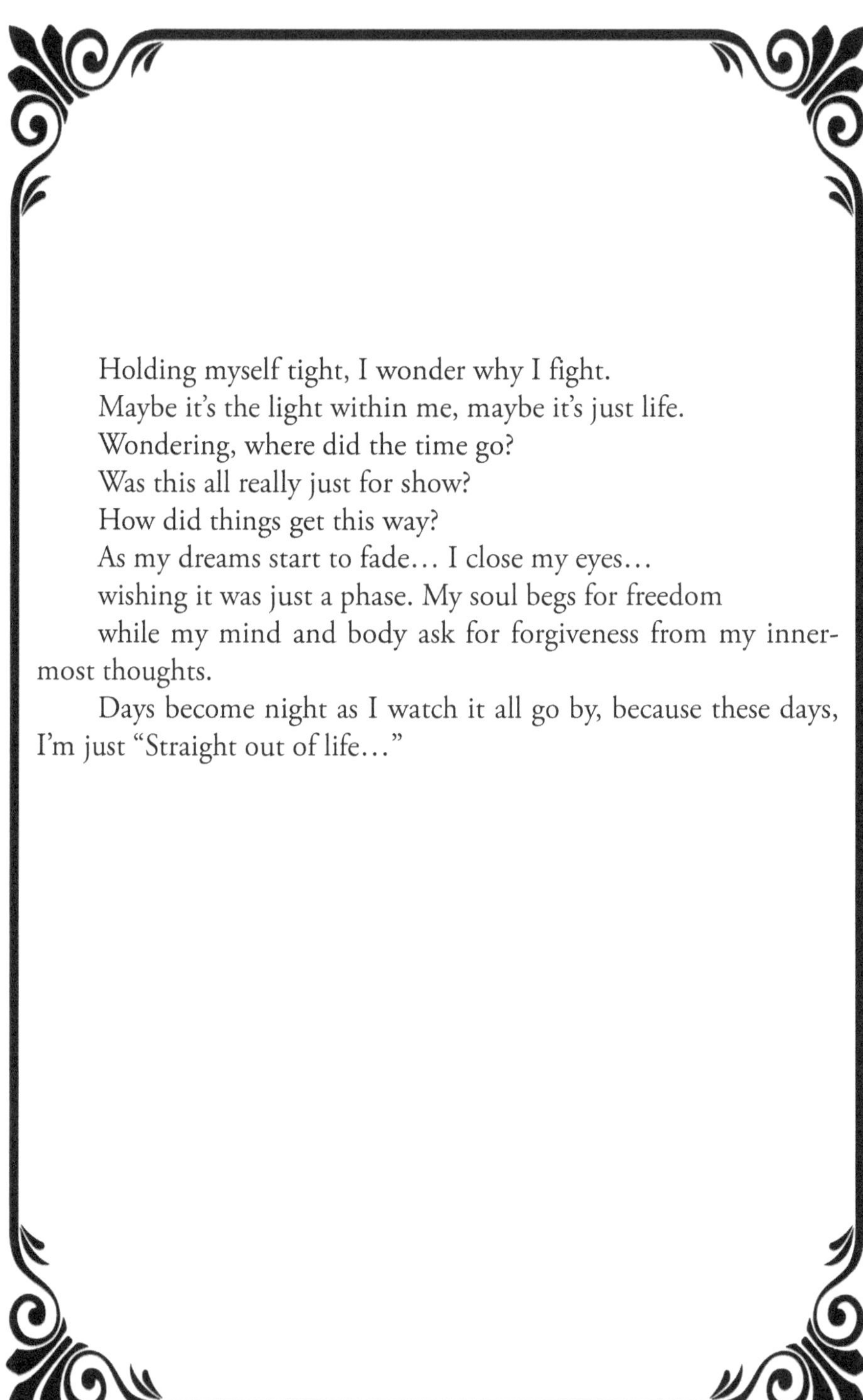

Holding myself tight, I wonder why I fight.
Maybe it's the light within me, maybe it's just life.
Wondering, where did the time go?
Was this all really just for show?
How did things get this way?
As my dreams start to fade… I close my eyes…
wishing it was just a phase. My soul begs for freedom
while my mind and body ask for forgiveness from my inner-most thoughts.

Days become night as I watch it all go by, because these days, I'm just "Straight out of life…"

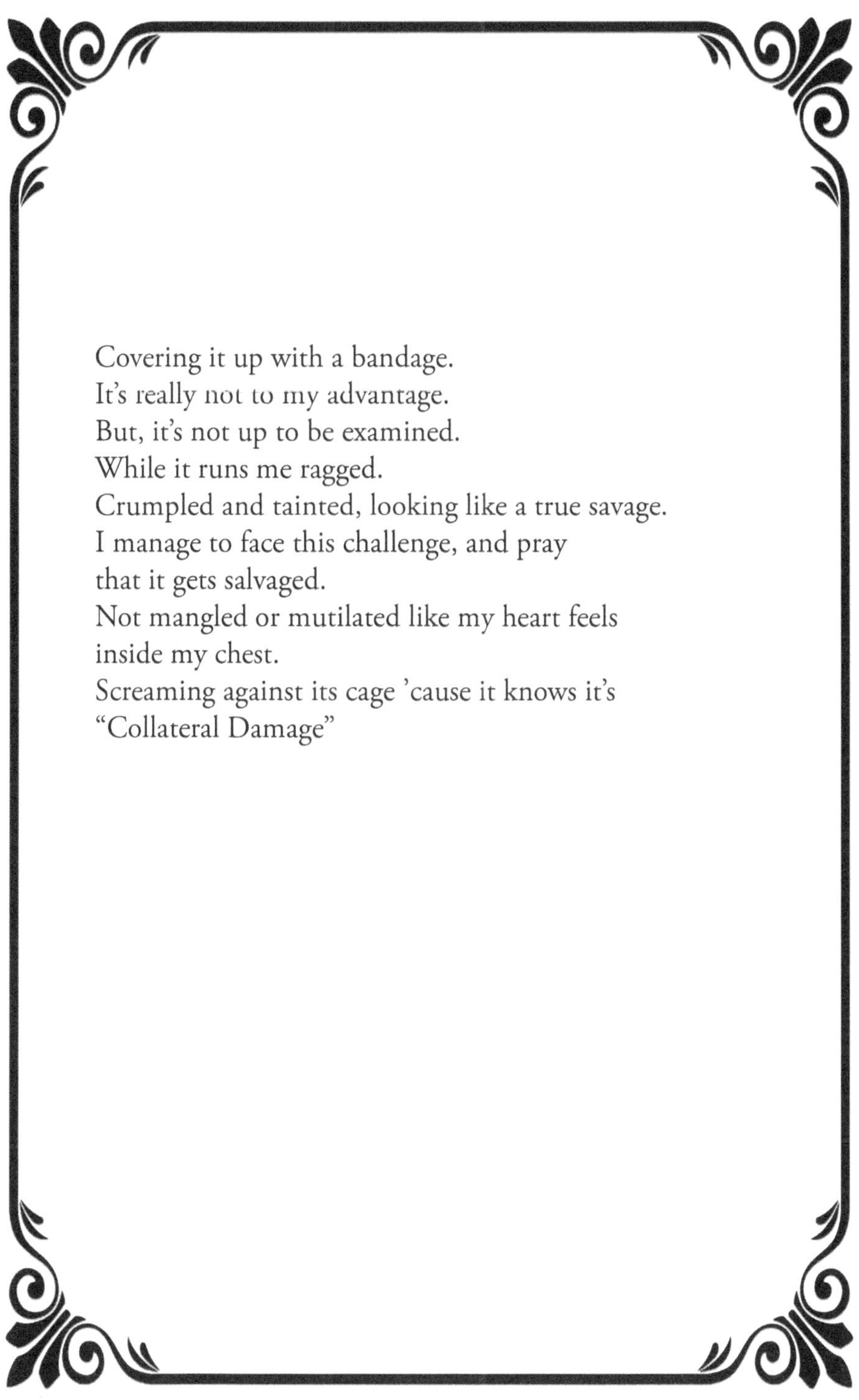

Covering it up with a bandage.
It's really not to my advantage.
But, it's not up to be examined.
While it runs me ragged.
Crumpled and tainted, looking like a true savage.
I manage to face this challenge, and pray
that it gets salvaged.
Not mangled or mutilated like my heart feels
inside my chest.
Screaming against its cage 'cause it knows it's
"Collateral Damage"

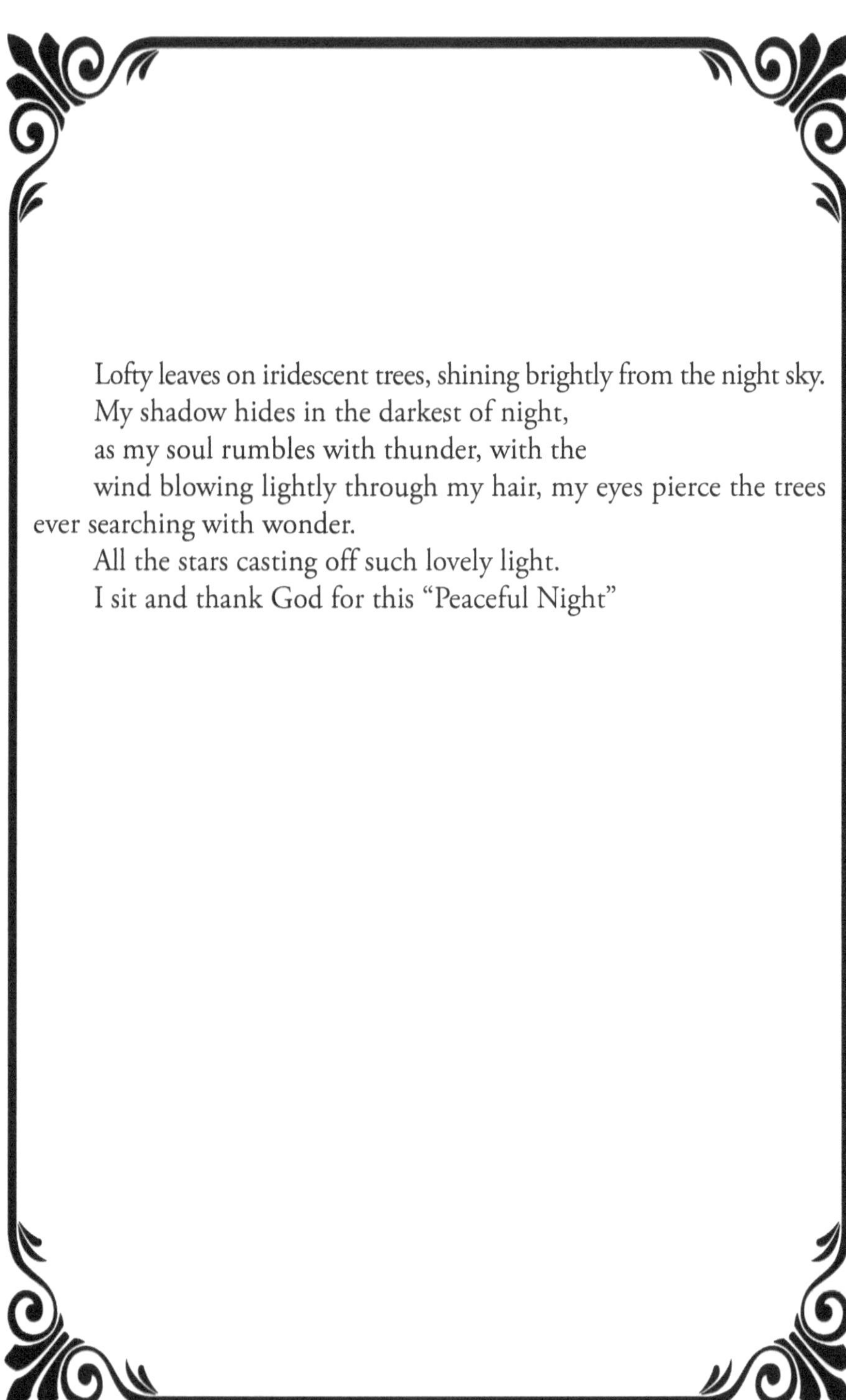

Lofty leaves on iridescent trees, shining brightly from the night sky.
My shadow hides in the darkest of night,
as my soul rumbles with thunder, with the
wind blowing lightly through my hair, my eyes pierce the trees
ever searching with wonder.
All the stars casting off such lovely light.
I sit and thank God for this "Peaceful Night"

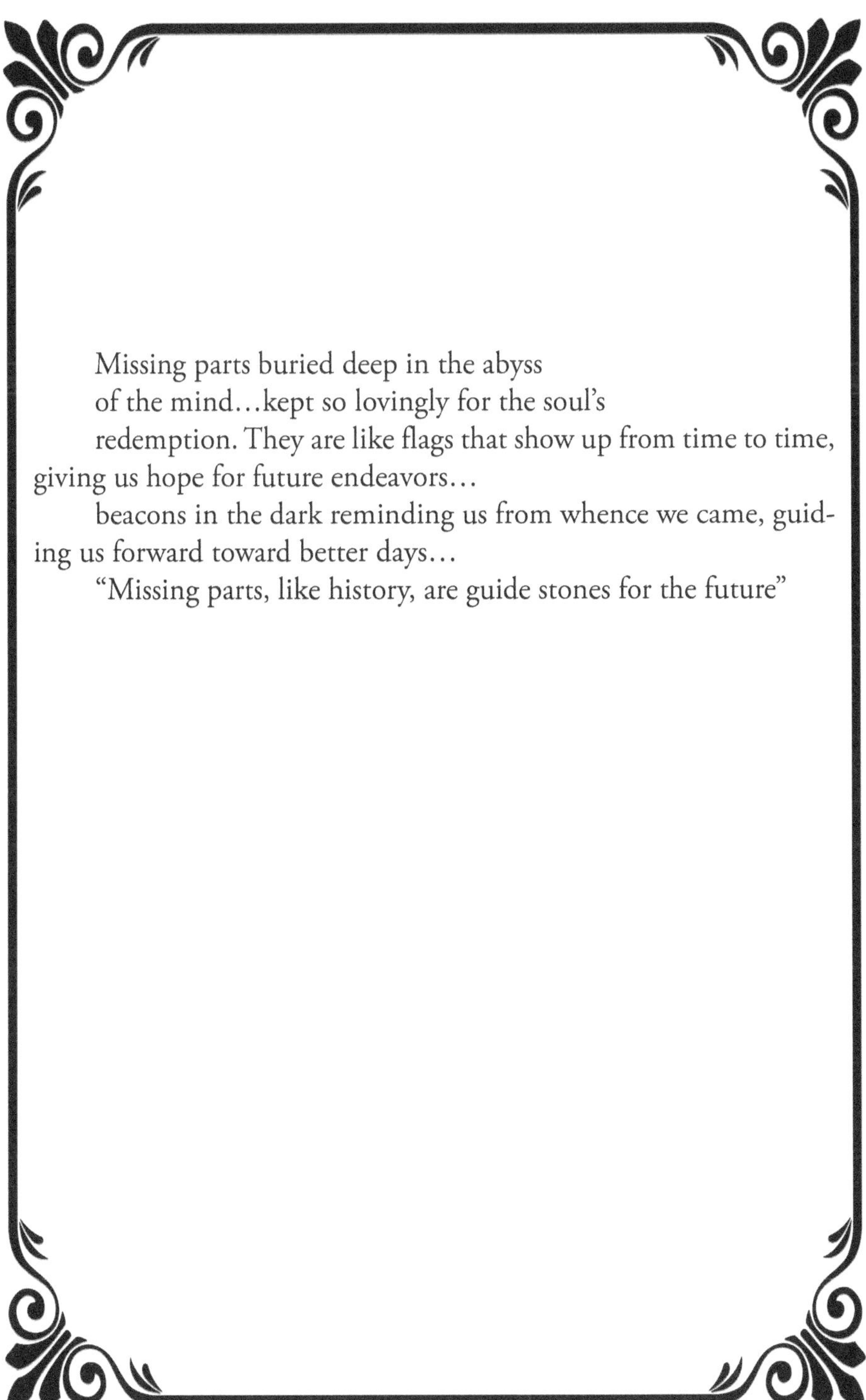

Missing parts buried deep in the abyss
of the mind…kept so lovingly for the soul's
redemption. They are like flags that show up from time to time,
giving us hope for future endeavors…
beacons in the dark reminding us from whence we came, guiding us forward toward better days…
"Missing parts, like history, are guide stones for the future"

When all looks faded, and everything seems
in despair… Your dreams are still there!

You see them in your mind, you envision them so clear! Taking the leap seems dire, but you err on the side of caution…waiting for that push, that acceptance that you are allowed…it doesn't come, so you stay where you are waiting…and dreaming, but in reality, you should jump and grab it because believing in yourself is "Seeing the Impossible"

My world hurts, and my heart bleeds the pain…
through my eyes, it leaks down my face.

Dropping heavy on my chest, like thunder in the sky… My heart still beats even though it bleeds for the world so openly! Often unnoticed, and left to myself, to patch up the hurts…

Trying to live life anew, giving it my all for better days ahead. Battered hearts bleed for the world openly, so boldly courageous are openhearted souls.

"Haggard devotion brings the soul new life"

How my heart breaks to rise with the sun…

spilling its blood through the tears washing down my face! Running through my soul with bare feet,

and long paces…holding my breath waiting for the release! Like the rising sun, my heart bursts with emotions, no longer able to hold them in this cage… I rise up with the sun, like the phoenix from the fire!

"Ashes forged from the Blaze"

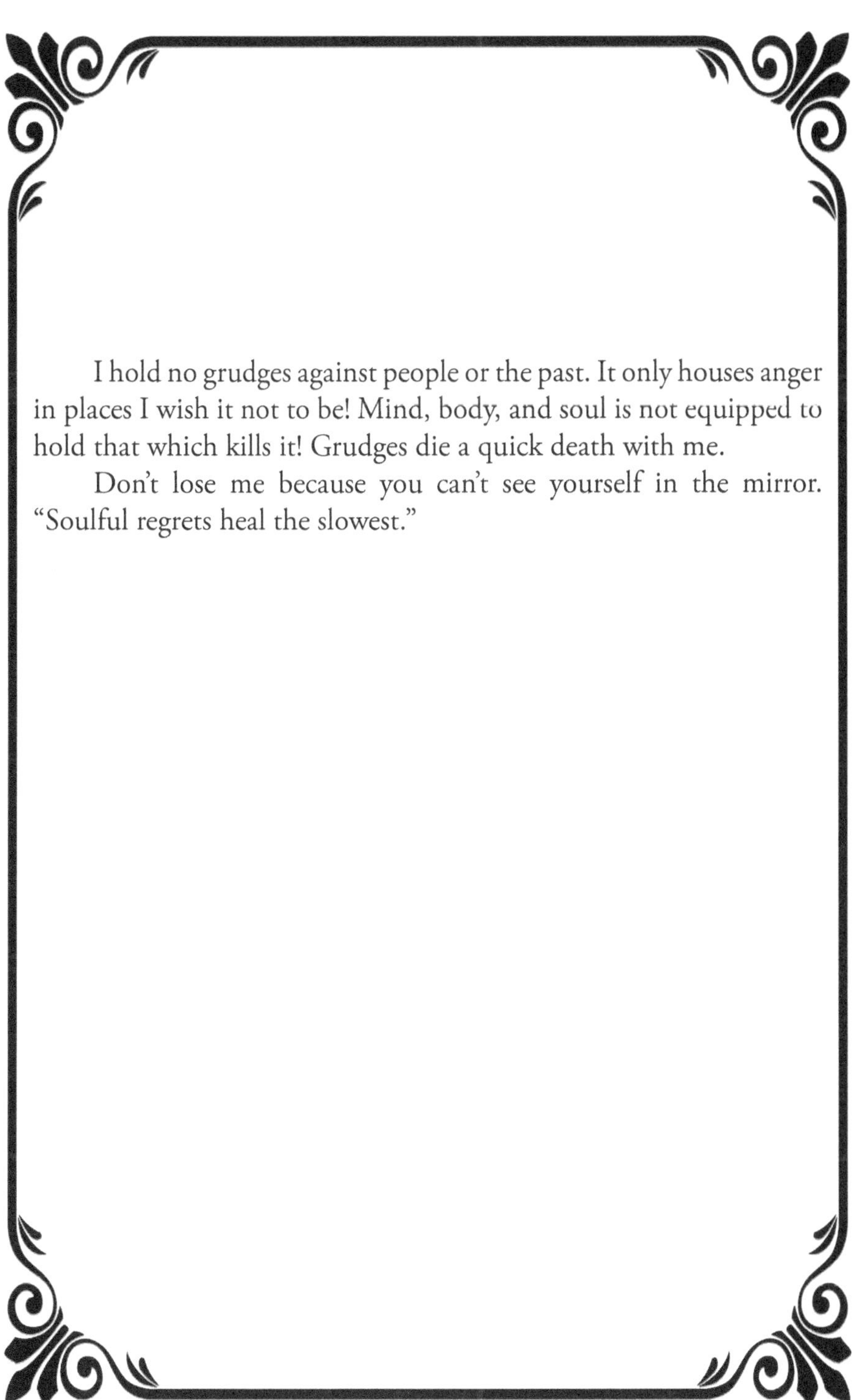

I hold no grudges against people or the past. It only houses anger in places I wish it not to be! Mind, body, and soul is not equipped to hold that which kills it! Grudges die a quick death with me.

Don't lose me because you can't see yourself in the mirror. "Soulful regrets heal the slowest."

When you focus on the enemy, you give away your growth for free! Growth takes strength, which the enemy doesn't deserve.

Don't let years fly by giving away your strength and growth to the ones that don't appreciate it enough to acknowledge that you are doing it.

It takes years' worth of joy from your soul, and ages you prematurely.

"Aging with the enemy takes life from your years."

Sometimes you have to be quiet to see clearly…
"Quiet sight brings Clarity"

These words are short and lonely like the insecurities deep inside my mind. Don't worry, little ones, we will be as big and heavy like this heart inside its cage! As beautiful as building a brick wall… one brick, two brick, three! As tall and mighty as the day is long. Standing beautiful overlooking all…

Time flies by and the wall still stands…beautifully suffering in society as the will inside crumbles! Sometimes shells are just shells, and they need to be filled with hope and all things good, until they are no longer "Suffering in Society"

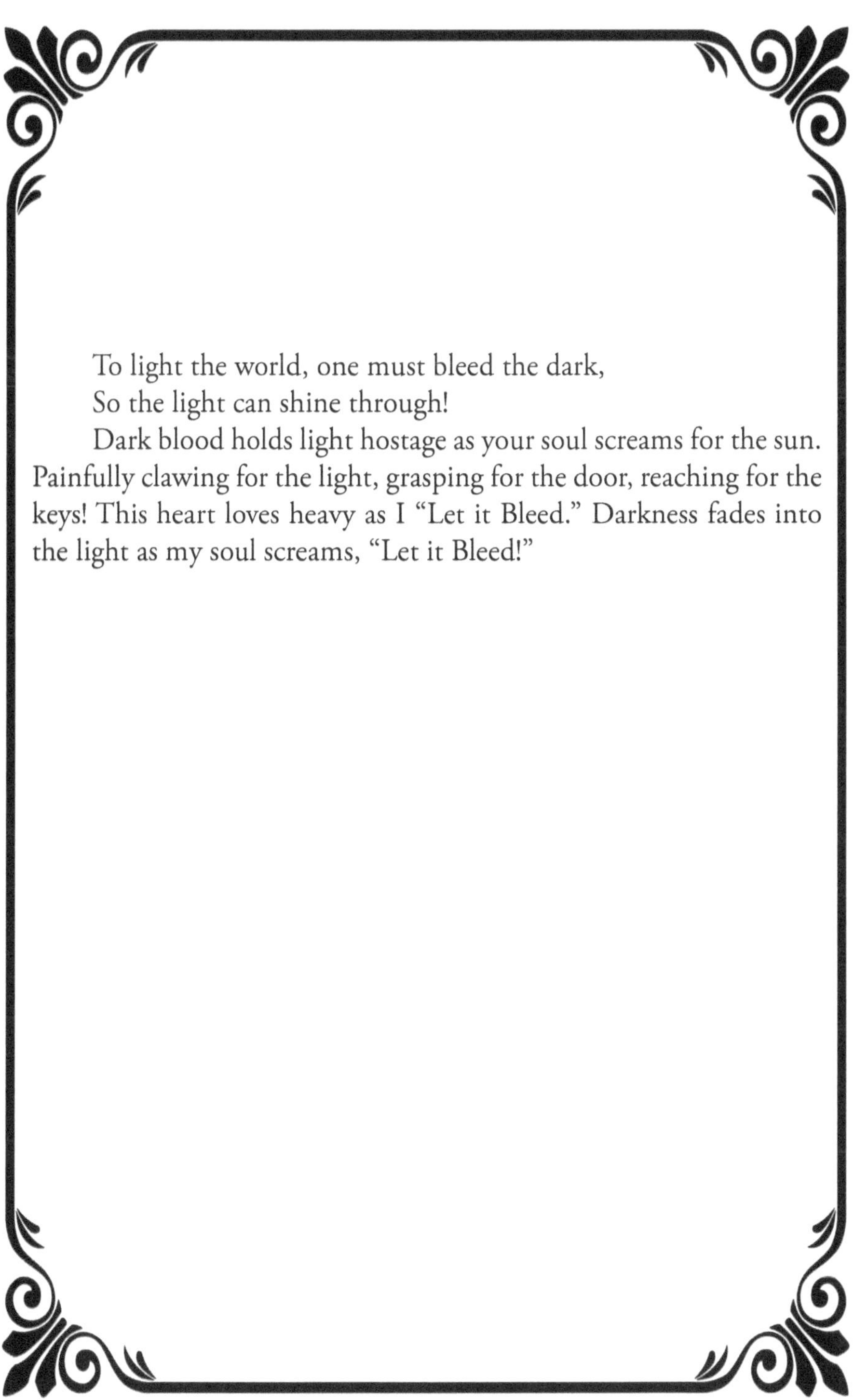

To light the world, one must bleed the dark,
So the light can shine through!
Dark blood holds light hostage as your soul screams for the sun. Painfully clawing for the light, grasping for the door, reaching for the keys! This heart loves heavy as I "Let it Bleed." Darkness fades into the light as my soul screams, "Let it Bleed!"

Long-suffering never sails a ship in tormented seas… Rough water rolling deep within the tattered soul blows holes in the sail-cloth like bullets fired from a gun… Dying for perspective leaves the heart wide-open! Love the empty spaces and sail the high seas! Rough waters make life seem easy…

"Live vivaciously with level satiny"

My faith is bigger than the enemy's gates. I hold the key when I see the gates as stepping-stones instead of stopping points. Dedication only works when you cast away self-doubt. Easier said than done are these. Courage doesn't come easy, and love never hurt anyone. Love your courage to have faith in yourself to break the enemy's gates, and step easy down the stones of dedication to your goals in life! "The enemy's gates" don't break us, our own self-doubt does that.

Love your lamppost. It's beautiful in the night! Shining brightly for the lost, downtrodden, and worried. We as lights are beacons for others when the world is in need. Even when we ourselves are dim, we can still hold light for the next. Sometimes that may be the only light one sees in a sea of darkness! Giving them hope that they will make it another day. Love your light, and love your lamppost. It's a beacon in the night, and it's beautiful to the world!

Awake in a world of sleepless nights, burning through the midnight fire…my eyes see none while my thoughts hear everything. This is how my soul works through the wilderness of the world's problems that lie on my heart with the heaviness of gold and the sorrows of the raven! Pandora never knew her maker before she gave out her demons! We burn the "Midnight Fire" to get rid of the ash that trashes the soul! In the world's arms, we live out our problems, when all we need to do is "Burn the Midnight Fire"

When my voice runs out and the world is raging, sing the soul to the heavens, for it shall ring out and love the rage to quietness… Peaceful minds bring awareness of the day at hand! The present in all its wonders! The heart looks with eyes that are steady upon the faces of these that dare to dream…for better days are come to wash away the old! In memory we don't have to live harsh parts, but learn from them. History needs lived like the way we should love—"Truthfully aware of self"

Sold into the soul like time ticks away. Falling off the cliff, the dirt crashes below. Awareness hits like bricks on the chest, strong and steadfast! Sold on the day we break into the mind…leaving of consciousness grasping for the why! Only to realize it's loved us all along. The breath of life leaves us wanting when all we need is to let it breathe…loving the breath that our soul already knew we needed. "Sold in the Soul" is our heart's only hope.

Humane doesn't have an expiration date…
We do…

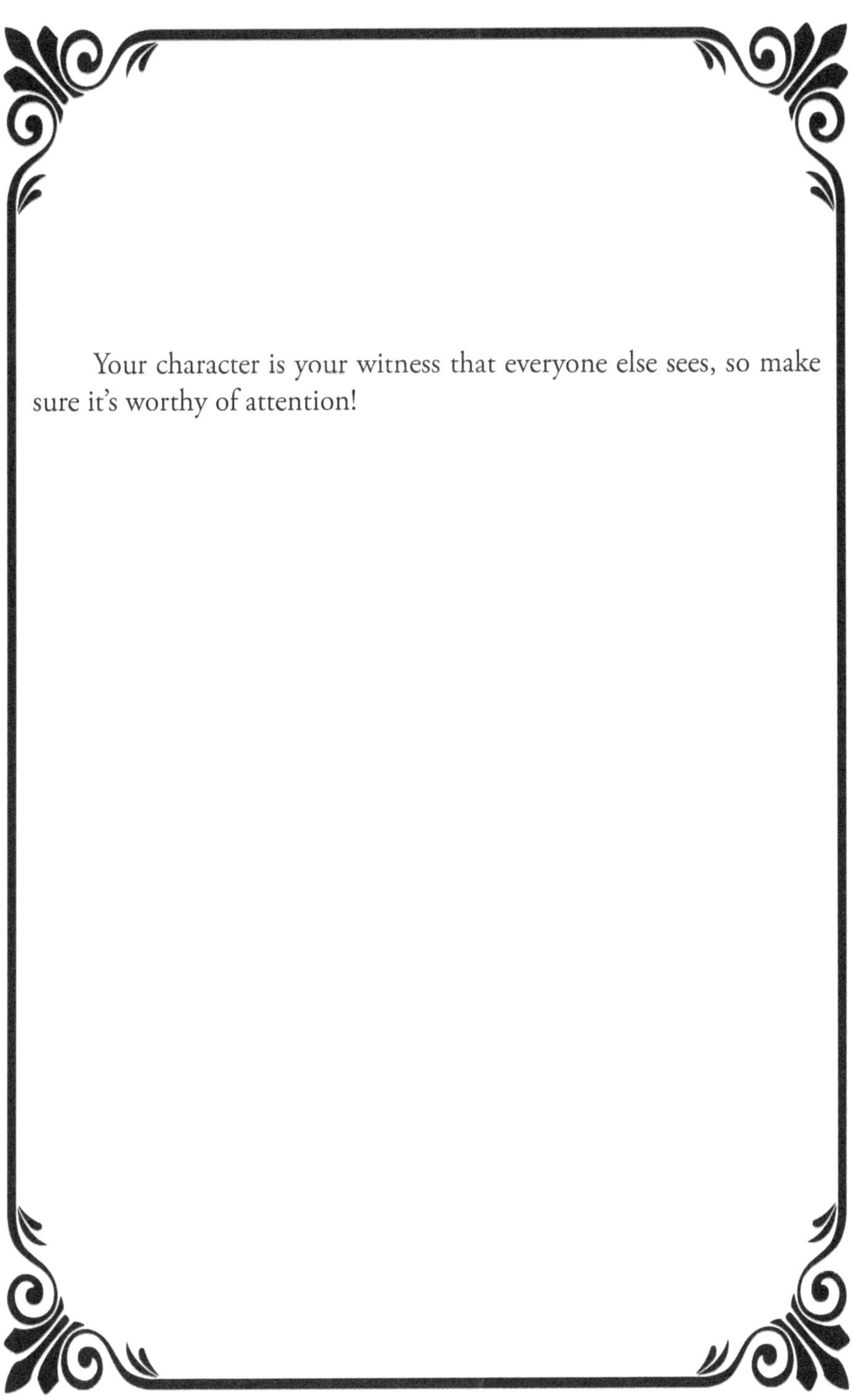

Your character is your witness that everyone else sees, so make sure it's worthy of attention!

Don't be jealous of someone that decided to step up to the plate when you didn't! Fortitude comes at a cost, and empathy serves it well. Being human means living a lesson. "Justice in Empathy"

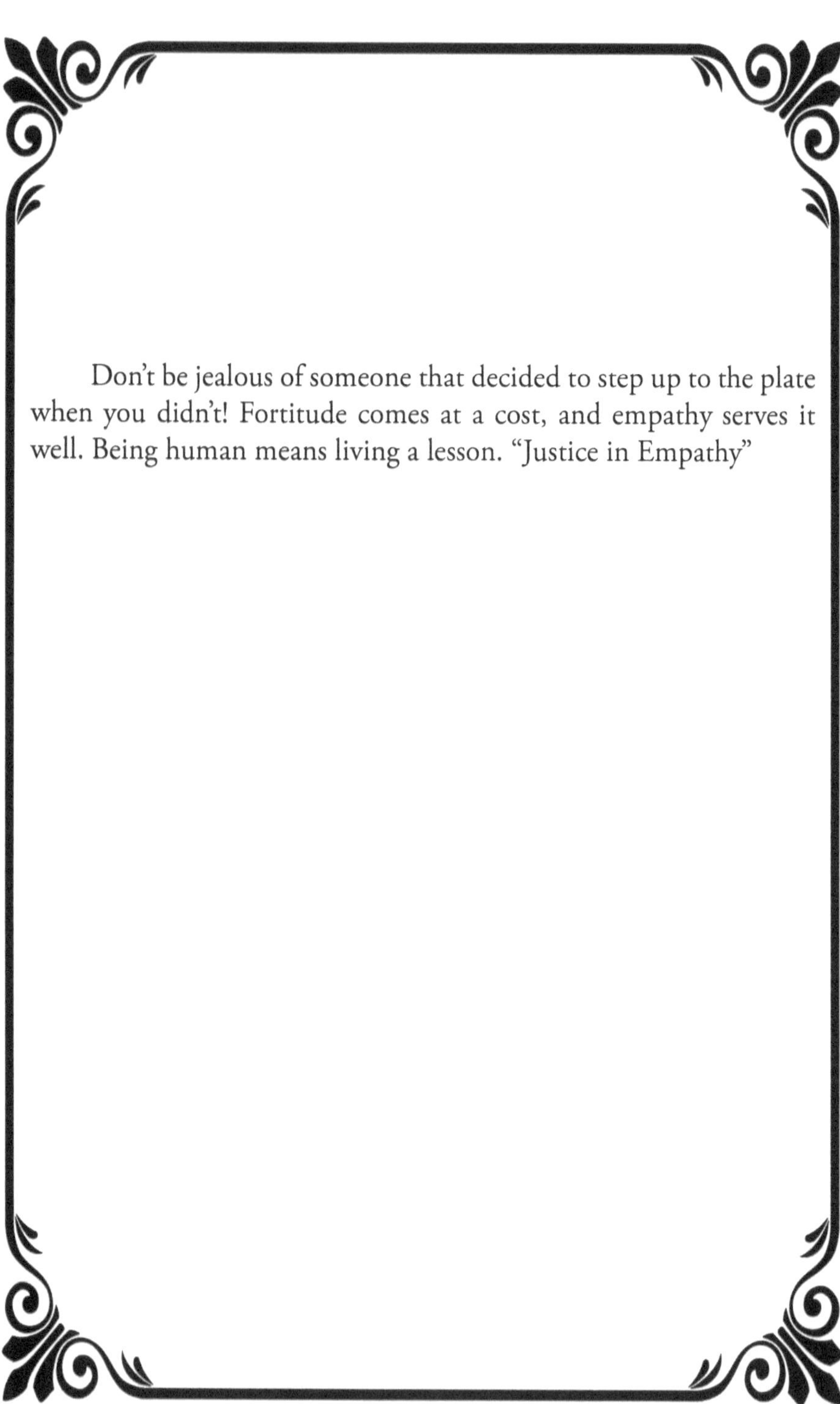

Cutthroat and ruthless, eventually makes a thinking man… Intellect sometimes comes with a price! Bruised and bloody, man's favorite way to pass a test. Lessons learned through hell's gates bring you closer to your soul's best sight! Seeing twenty-twenty is heavy when you don't listen…

While the world is raging against its own self, we watch the dying. Hoping that the rage will save them from ourselves…only to see the death! In vain, we live fighting the cause of our own doing, but nothing gets accomplished because the tug rope never moves! It's time to drop the rope and change directions! Moving toward a life that's "worth the death!" Surrender the death so the world can live!

We are not the darkness in the dying light. We are the light giving way… Darkness has its place in the world. It's when the light rests and we renew ourselves for the coming day. For all the world, we shine for the peace of it. Hope breaks way in the rested soul. Peace surrenders the world in love when we let ourselves be the light that gives hope. The soul that lives so others can breathe… Without breath, we cease to exist, and without love, we are abandoned! "We are the dying light." Let us love you so your soul lives in the peace of it!

Life is not linear, no matter how much we want it to be. It's a series of twists and turns, like pretzels. One part of the path may loop over another. Lessons innate and filtered through our being to be learned with prowess! Hope never dies on courageous souls, but lives high upon the seas of love, which conquers all. Gifts among us in the teacher's eyes! "Lessons give us strength, While courage builds us."

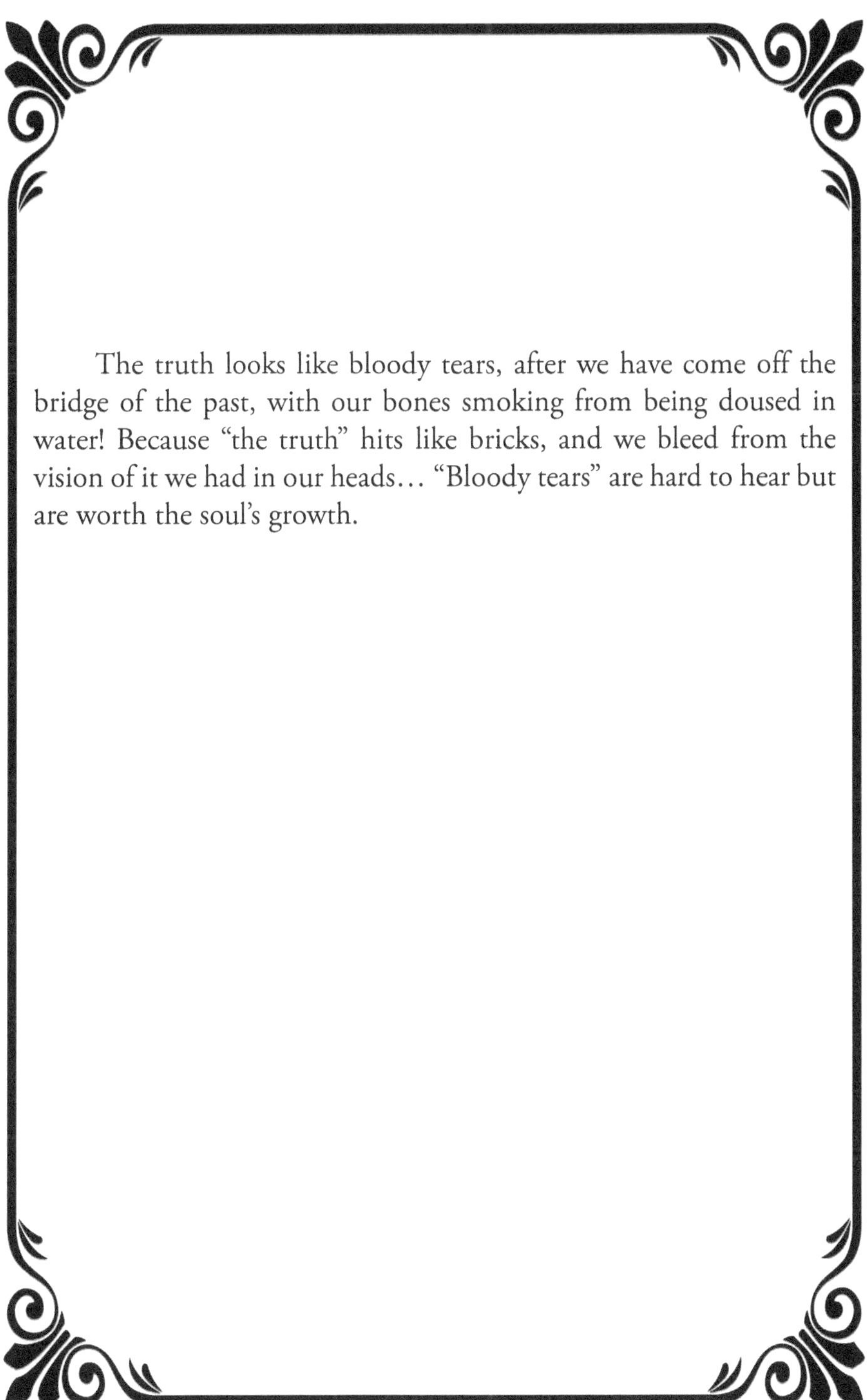

The truth looks like bloody tears, after we have come off the bridge of the past, with our bones smoking from being doused in water! Because "the truth" hits like bricks, and we bleed from the vision of it we had in our heads… "Bloody tears" are hard to hear but are worth the soul's growth.

Never ask permission to use your own power. It doesn't belong to them, so they have no authority to tell you whether you can use it or not. They can only ask you if they can plug into it or not. Your power belongs to you, and is not of any other's consequence! It's only broken if we allow it. The power within lives inside us all. "Power of being" lives through our actions, and it's up to us to make them worthy.

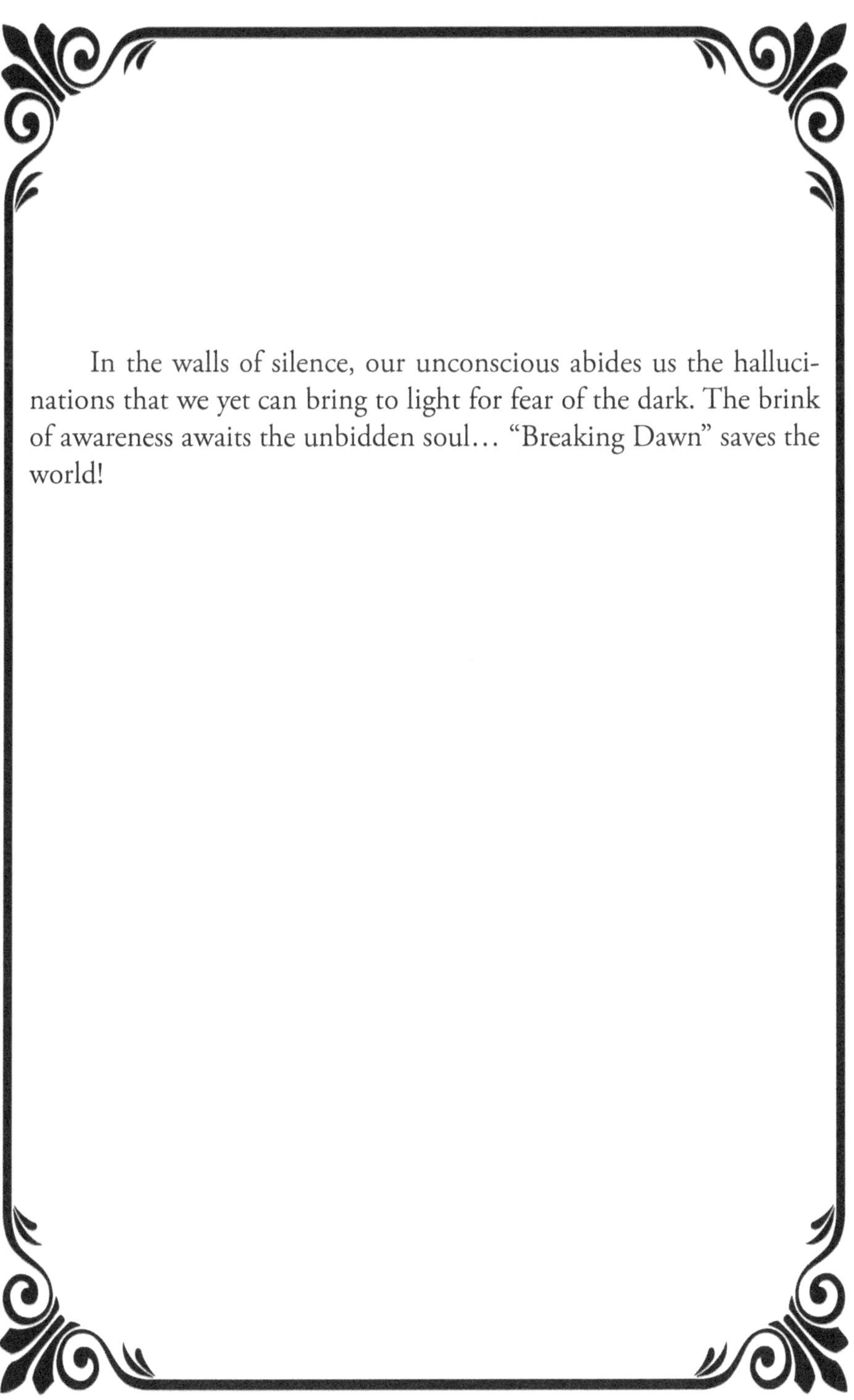

In the walls of silence, our unconscious abides us the hallucinations that we yet can bring to light for fear of the dark. The brink of awareness awaits the unbidden soul… "Breaking Dawn" saves the world!

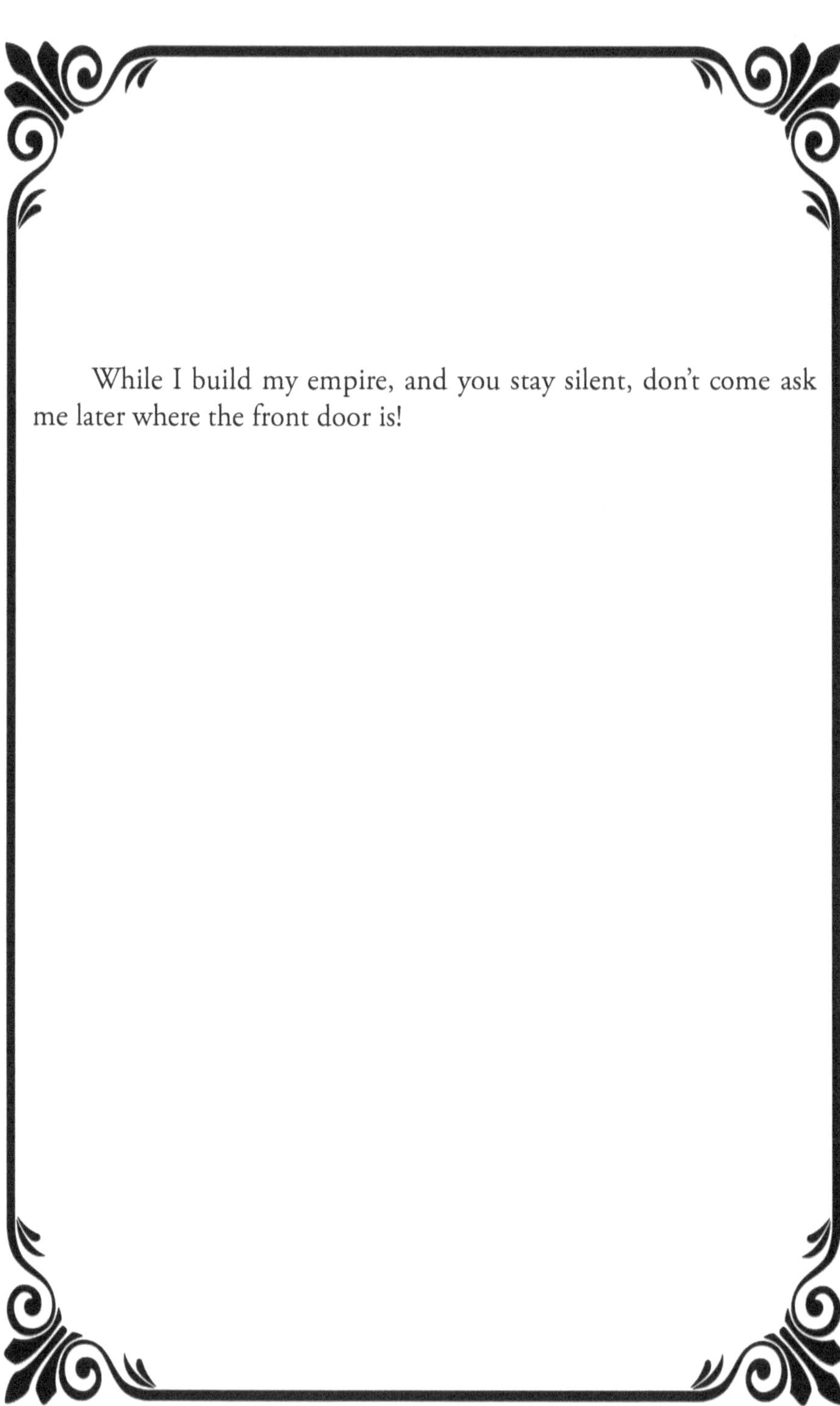

While I build my empire, and you stay silent, don't come ask me later where the front door is!

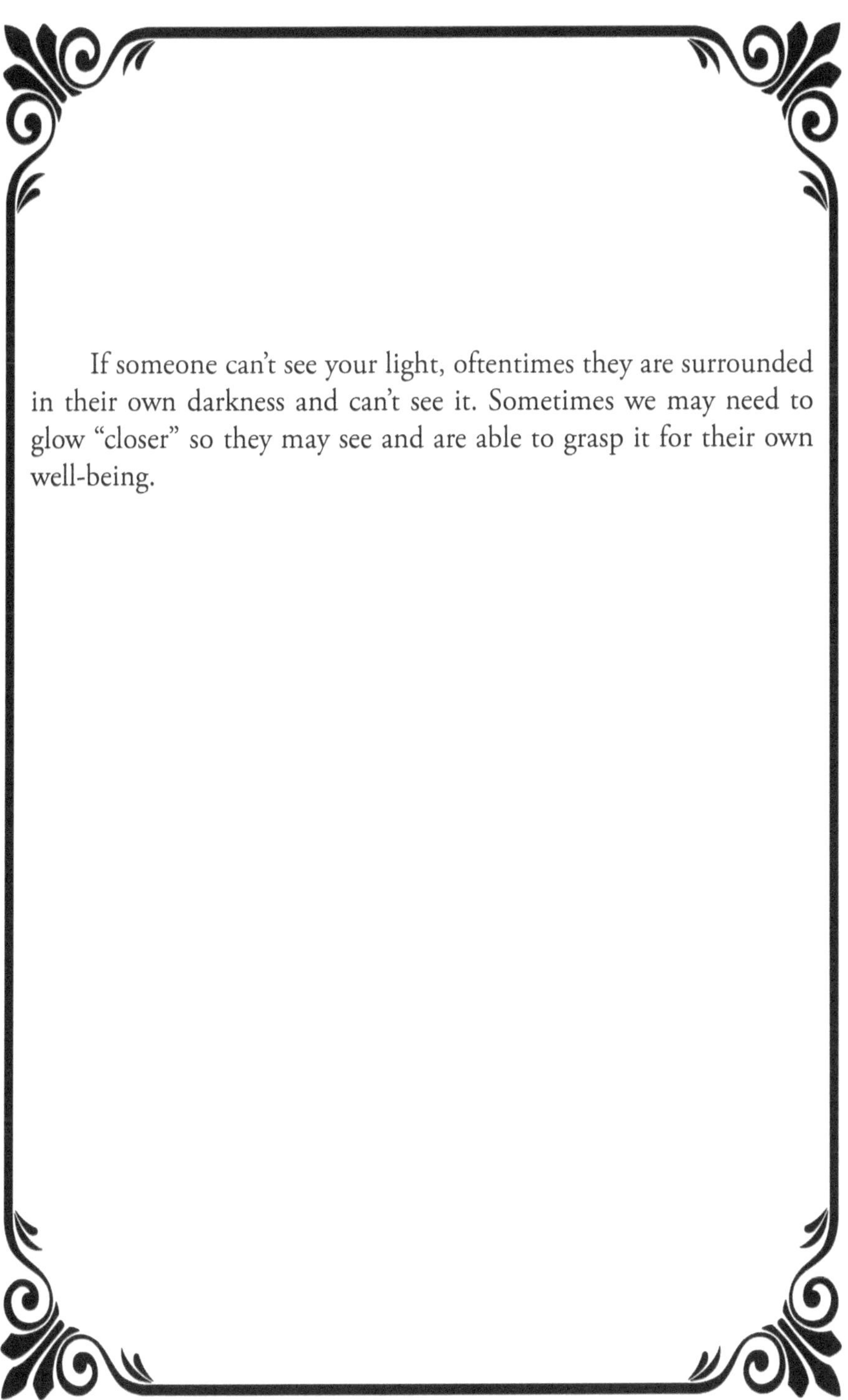

If someone can't see your light, oftentimes they are surrounded in their own darkness and can't see it. Sometimes we may need to glow "closer" so they may see and are able to grasp it for their own well-being.

What you say to none speaks volumes to many. On deaf ears we scream…only to impale ourselves on knives we didn't throw! "Open minds don't throw knives," and we don't bleed all over them… "Living openly is love unconditional!"

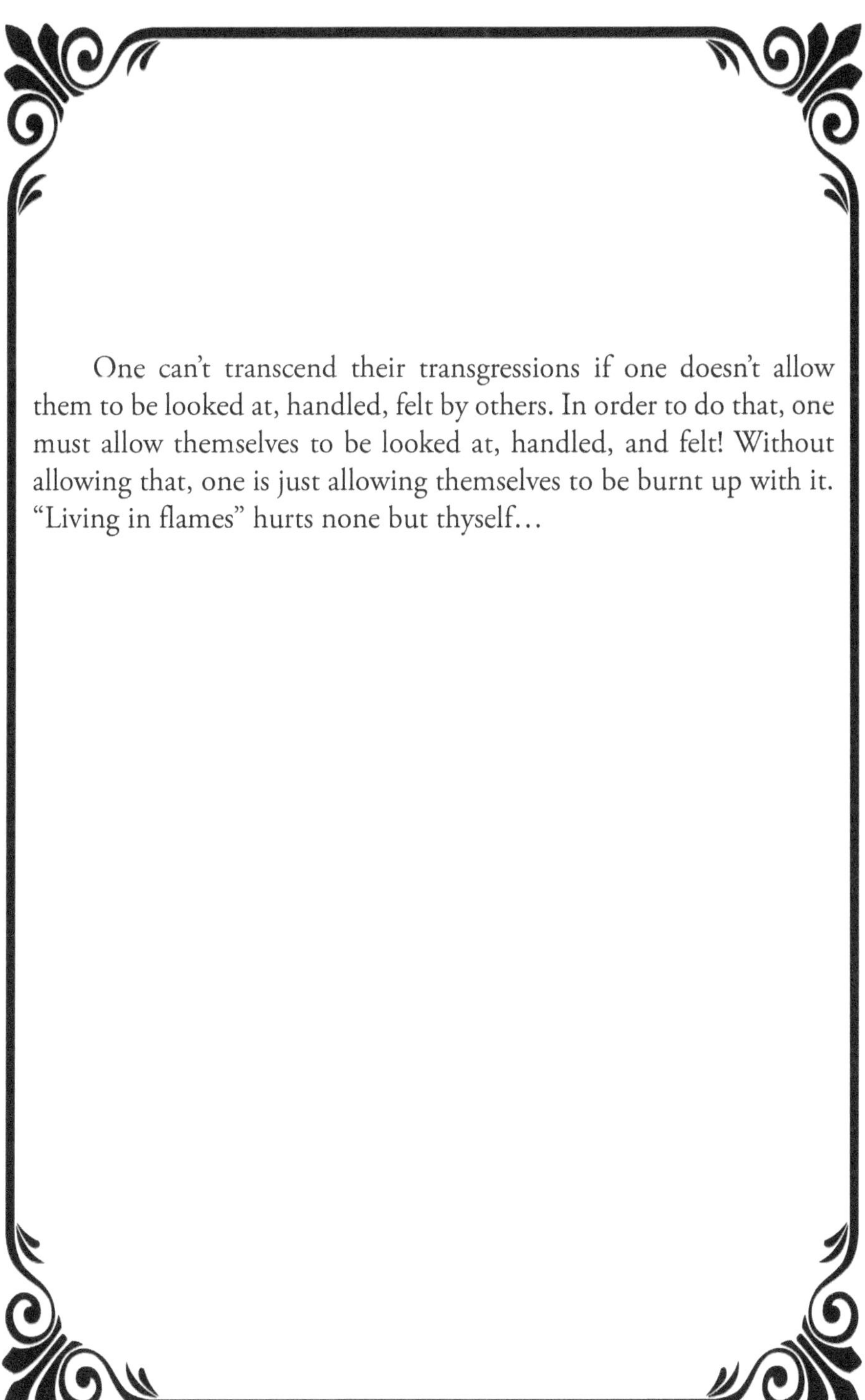

One can't transcend their transgressions if one doesn't allow them to be looked at, handled, felt by others. In order to do that, one must allow themselves to be looked at, handled, and felt! Without allowing that, one is just allowing themselves to be burnt up with it. "Living in flames" hurts none but thyself…

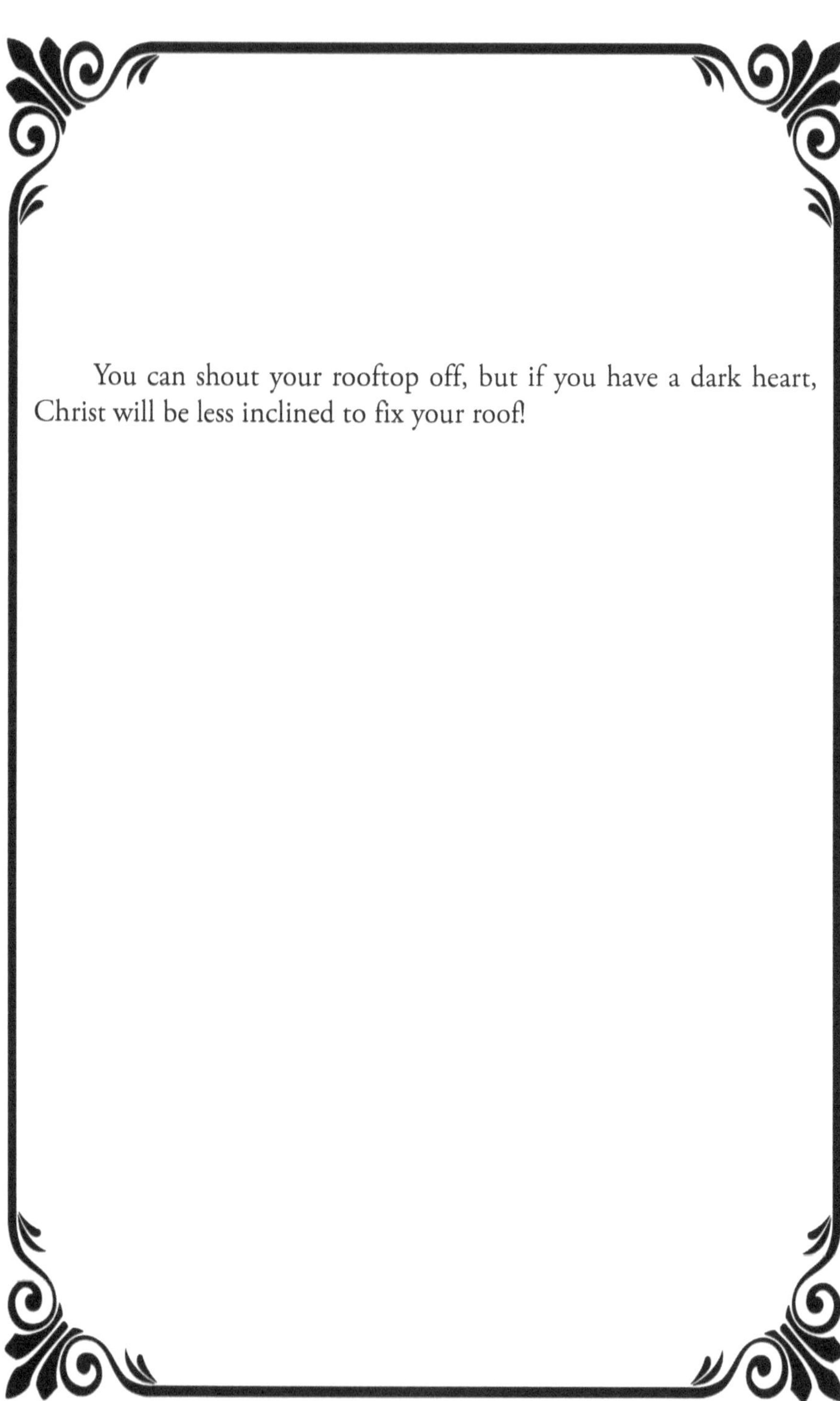

You can shout your rooftop off, but if you have a dark heart, Christ will be less inclined to fix your roof!

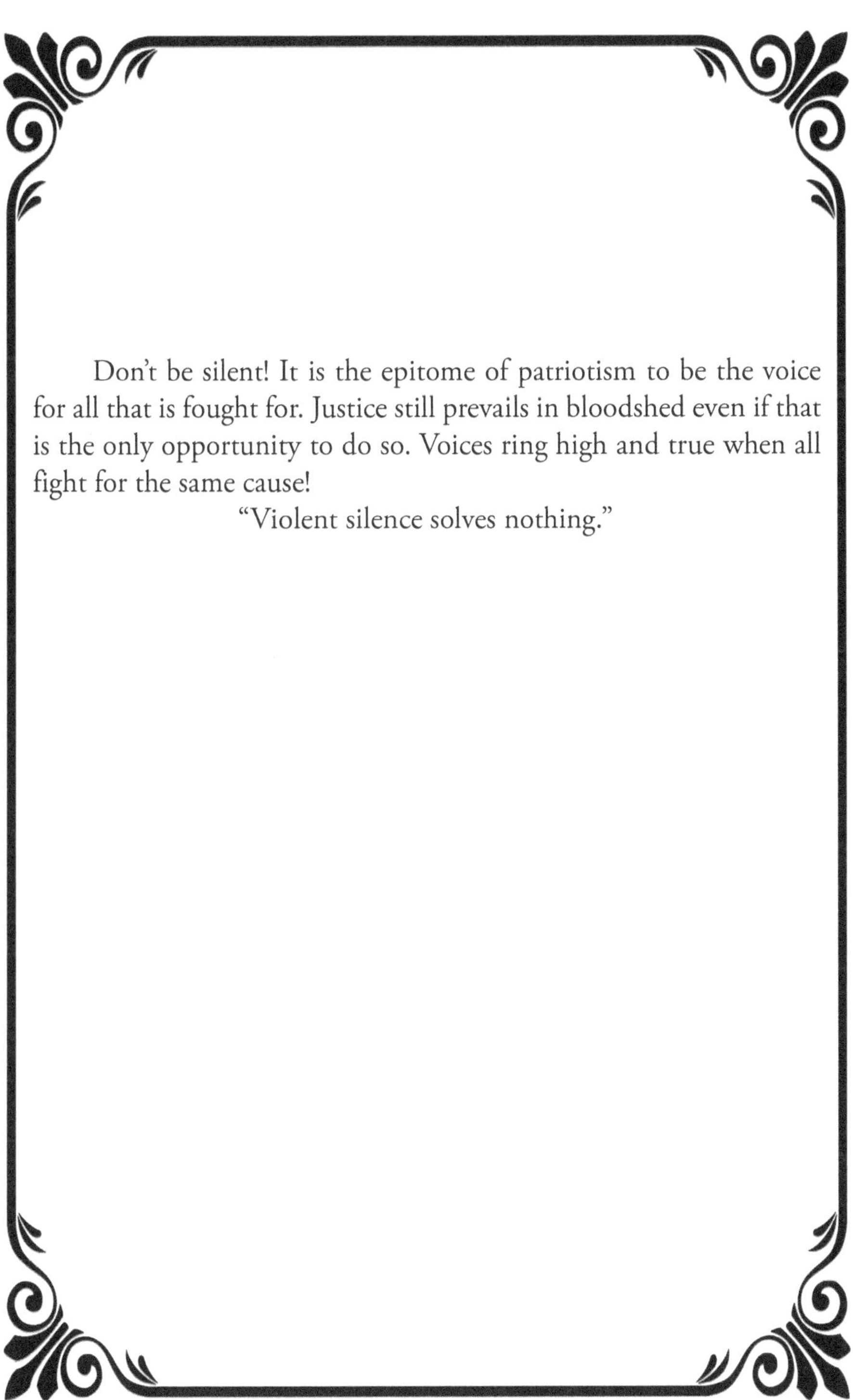

Don't be silent! It is the epitome of patriotism to be the voice for all that is fought for. Justice still prevails in bloodshed even if that is the only opportunity to do so. Voices ring high and true when all fight for the same cause!

"Violent silence solves nothing."

When you fight for freedom, your soul speaks against its oppression. What you feel that quakes inside, rumbling against the inside of your body like an earthquake! Rolling like thunder, waiting for the right time to strike. "Freedom calms the soul like rushing water carves a river."

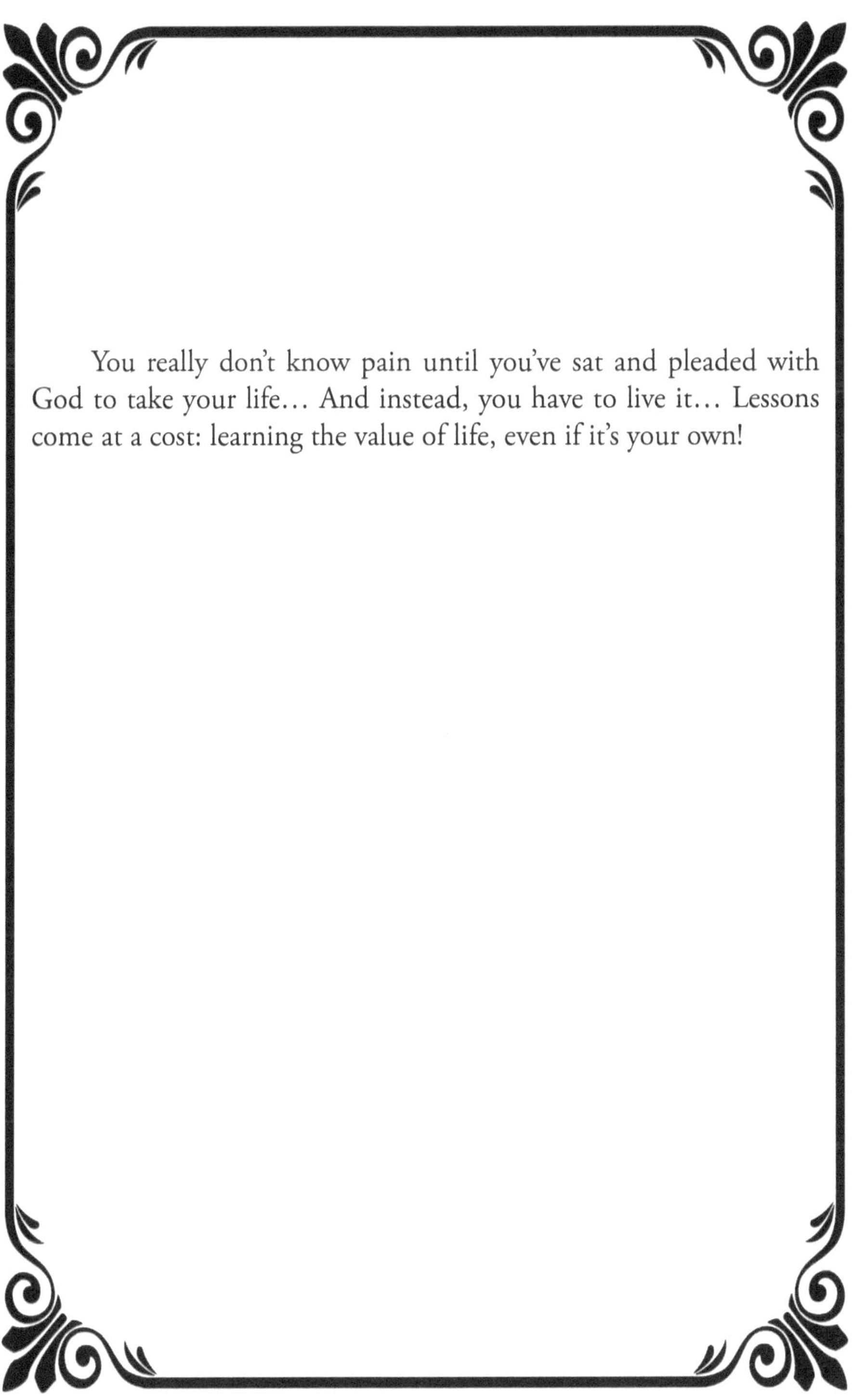

You really don't know pain until you've sat and pleaded with God to take your life… And instead, you have to live it… Lessons come at a cost: learning the value of life, even if it's your own!

It is the essence of being human to err on the side of caution when it comes to seeing our truth. Our conscience makes us aware of this truth, but most times, we choose not to follow it. It is of utmost importance that we do follow our inner truth! Open mine eyes and see the absolute… "Truth seeks the eye of the beholder" to live in light for all to "see." Live lively like "Third eye awake."

Every bit of strength comes from understanding that your soul is not separate from you, but as one. It lives as you do, and gives strength in times of adversity. Why we treat it as if it doesn't matter is beyond me! What resonates within, resonates with you. We can't live beyond its means, life doesn't work that way for long… Baring our soul to live life fully gives purpose to what is ingrained! Living whole with the soul shows the understanding the world needs! "Understand the whole of it"—the world needs more of that.

There is no misstep without a forward step. We can't misstep if we are standing still. Missteps often lead you in the direction you are supposed to be going. The path through life isn't straight and narrow, but more often wide and tangled. Living in the tangles builds character for the prize! Love your missteps, it's better than falling. "Living on the misstep brings lessons from the heart" and keeps our souls true to ourselves.

We don't get through this life without help… Seek the helpers! Watch them, see what they do. That's what we should all strive to be, a helper. Helpers give so effortlessly, it's in the blood. Humanity deserves to be helped. We deserve it. As humans, we try to do it all ourselves, it's a trauma response. Empathy brings life the love that humanity deserves! Be a "Helper" with an empathetic heart. Humanity will love you for it. "Help humanity love itself." Seek the helpers!

You cannot perceive the day if your heart is always dark. Those dungeons encase us like cement newly poured… If only we breathe and exhale the dark can we truly break the concrete walls and crawl out of the dungeon. Broken but yet whole! Hearts don't lie when it touches the light…giving way to our true selves! We are "Broken yet whole" from loving the light. Dark hearts die in our "Whole Brokenness."

Chaos reveals the damaged heart. In the surroundings of charred remains, you can see the hurt splattered everywhere. A person's brokenness is provoked when you touch the open wounds without regard or permission. What you receive from that encounter isn't always beautiful. Sometimes it's war. No one seems safe anymore, because we all have wounds, and no one asks permission anymore… While we stand in charred remains, we should endeavor to ourselves to ask permission! "When chaos reveals a damaged heart, ask permission!"

Walk the fire through the flames! Burn me beautiful with ash and cinders! Brave me human with a soul like the Phoenix! Flames sear life with soot that bleeds from the eyes! Crisp the edges of the soul like a well-worked sword! Breathe the wings of the back so high in the sky!

"We walk the fire because life calls the Phoenix!"

Walk the fire and breathe life! Phoenix, take flight with flaming wings, the soul beckons the sky as we walk "The Fire."

Whispers in the sand paint a picture like an artist's hand. Smooth with rough edges that form the land. Like time in an hourglass, we blow across the band of mountains, giving the sound of soft hands loving the world with hearts like home. Soulful wondering across the plains of time, through the hourglass we look with curious eyes at all the wonderful things! Like "Whispers in the sand" we paint pictures like an artist's hand on everything we touch. So be gentle and kind with your "Whispers in the sand!"

You can't love my heart the way your sunset eyes burn my skin…

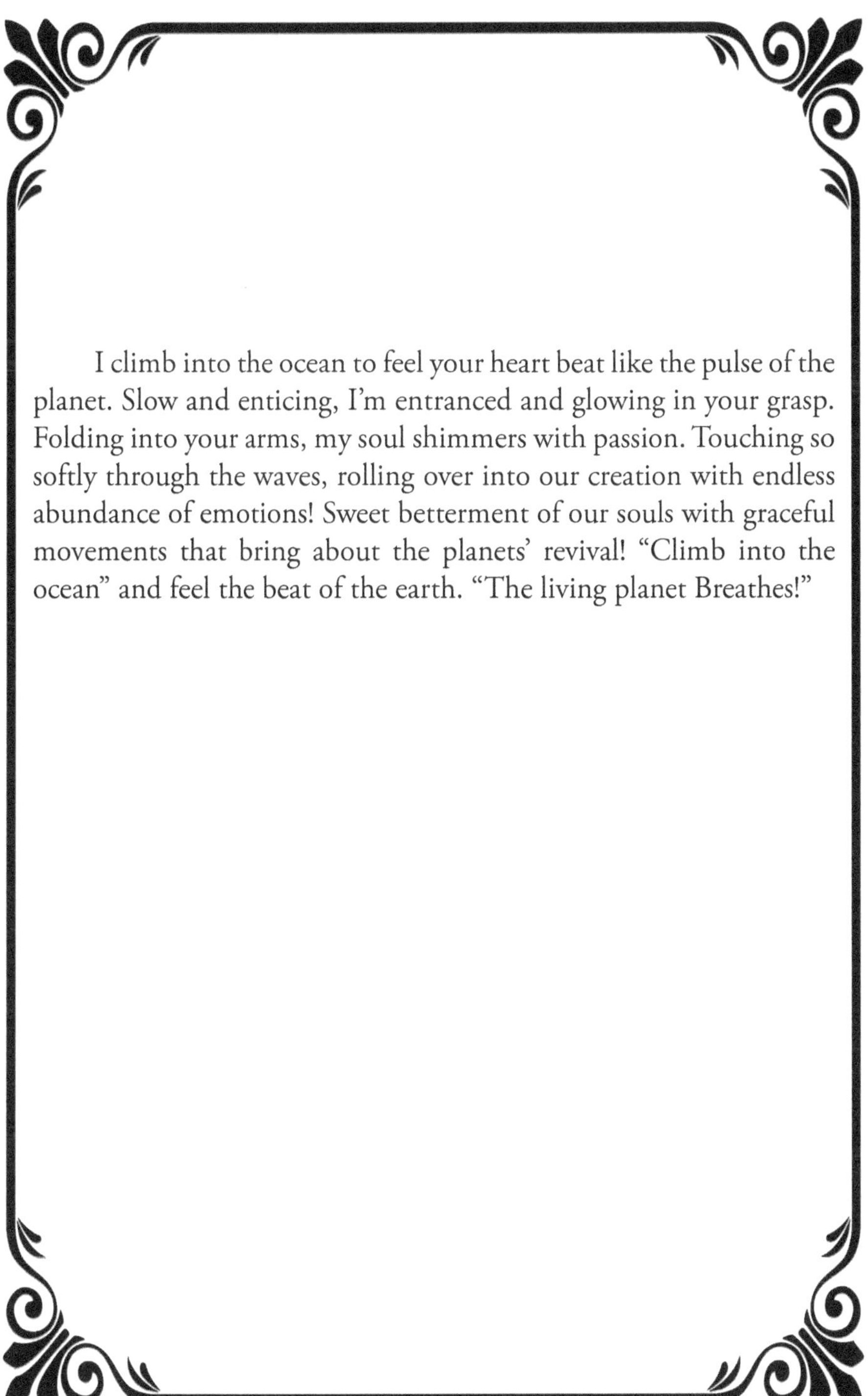

I climb into the ocean to feel your heart beat like the pulse of the planet. Slow and enticing, I'm entranced and glowing in your grasp. Folding into your arms, my soul shimmers with passion. Touching so softly through the waves, rolling over into our creation with endless abundance of emotions! Sweet betterment of our souls with graceful movements that bring about the planets' revival! "Climb into the ocean" and feel the beat of the earth. "The living planet Breathes!"

Let's get lost in effigies as we tear down our souls in lust for knowledge of the world! Statues in Solitude, with eyes that see through the dark into the light of the plains where the wild things live. Beating hearts run wild with compassion in their spirits, giving hope to the world when all looks bleak. Love bounds all when we get "lost in effigies!" So run wild like "Statues in Solitude."

Hang me from the stars so the light beats with you. Swim through space with me on the ship of tomorrow. Looking toward the future with bright eyes that only we can see…no longer languishing from the Dead Sea… Half-grown souls bright with intention, we tread lightly by the sun with its rays beaming widely! Ever so much faith in the depths of the universe that it captures me softly to "Hang me from the stars" so the light beats with me from mine eyes to yours; we drift through the dark sea of emotions so gleefully. Long are the days, gone from living in the Dead Sea…

I'm the quiet voice in the room screaming in my head. Reverberating in my head these dreams so far yet unfulfilled… Long wasted time, as the days pass me by. My heart longs for the days of peace of mind and no longer screaming but living the dreams that entice my soul! Writing on the wall for the world to see what lies in my heart… The beautiful mind breathes the words as my soul spells them out! "Living the screams lays down the purpose."

About the Author

Elizabeth Grundin is forty-three years old. She was born in the small Southern town of Fairhope, Alabama. She loves reading, writing, the arts, the outdoors, and many other things. She is interested in philosophy, science, space, and various other subjects. She is married and has one daughter and enjoys her family and friends. She loves the beach, searching for seashells, bodyboarding, listening to waves, and enjoying the sun. She loves nature and animals. Her love of life gives her inspiration. She has lived in the Florida Panhandle for the past twenty-five years. A Southerner at heart and lover of life, she thinks a lot and writes for all.

9 7 9 8 8 8 6 5 4 8 5 3 2